And the Beasts of the Field
had Respect unto him
and the Birds of the Air
were in no Fear of him,
for he made them not afraid,
yea even the wild Beasts of the Desert
perceived the Power of God in him,
and did him Service
bearing him from Place to Place.

Chapter 6, 14

Jesus'
Love for Animals

Christian Inspirations
from the
Gospel of the Holy Twelve

Bibliografische Information der Deutschen Nationalbibliothek:
Die Deutsche Nationalbibliothek verzeichnet diese Publikation in der Deutschen Nationalbibliografie; detaillierte bibliografische Daten sind im Internet über http://dnb.dnb.de abrufbar.

TWENTYSIX – Der Self-Publishing-Verlag
Eine Kooperation zwischen der Verlagsgruppe Random House und BoD – Books on Demand

© 2020 Antonia Katharina Tessnow

Herstellung und Verlag:
BoD – Books on Demand, Norderstedt

ISBN: 978-3-740-77148-5

English-language version by
Rev. Gideon Jasper Richard Ouseley M.A.

Writing, Format, Layout, Pictures, Punctuation Marks by
Antonia Katharina Tessnow

Website of the Author:
www.antonia-katharina.de

Verily, I tell you:
Whatever you did
to one of the Least of these,
my Brothers and Sisters,
you were doing it to me!

Matthew 25, 40

The Freeing of the Birds

And on a certain Day the Child Jesus came to a Place where a Snare was set for Birds, and there were some Boys there. And Jesus said to them: 'Who hath set this Snare for the innocent Creatures of God? Behold in a Snare, shall they in like manner be caught.' And he beheld twelve Sparrows as if they were dead.

And he moved his Hands over them, and said to them: 'Go, fly away, and while ye live, remember me.' And they arose and fled away making a Noise. And the Jews, seeing this, were astonished and told it unto the Priests.

Chapter 6, 7 - 8

Twistna Dog aus dem Alten Jagdhaus

Jesus brings Peace
between all Animals and Mankind

For the Spirit of Divine Humanity filling him, filled all Things around him, and made all Things subject unto him, and thus shall yet be fulfilled the Words of the Prophets: The Lion shall lie down with the Calf, and the Leopard with the Kid, and the Wolf with the Lamb, and the Bear with the Donkey, and the Owl with the Dove. And a Child shall lead them.

And none shall hurt or destroy on my holy Mountain, for the Earth shall be full of the Knowledge of the Holy One, even as the Waters cover the Bed of the Sea. And in that Day, I will make again a Covenant with the Beasts of the Earth and the Fowls of the Air, and the Fishes of the Sea and with all created Things. And will break the Bow and the Sword and all the Instruments of Warfare will I banish from the Earth, and will make them to lie down in safety, and to live without Fear.

Chapter 6, 15 - 16

Jesus delivereth a Lion from the Hunters

And on a certain Day, as he was passing by a Mountainside nigh unto the Desert, there met him a Lion and many Men were pursuing him with Stones and Javelins to slay him.

But Jesus rebuked them, saying: 'Why hunt ye these Creatures of God, which are more noble than you? By the Cruelties of many Generations, they were made the Enemies of Man, who should have been his Friends.

If the Power of God is shown in them, so also is shown his long Suffering and Compassion. Cease ye to persecute this Creature, who desireth not to harm you, see ye not how he fleeth from you, and is terrified by your Violence?'

And the Lion came and lay at the Feet of Jesus, and shewed Love to him; and the People were astonish, and said: 'Lo, this Man loveth all Creatures and hath Power to command even these Beasts from the Desert, and they obey him.'

Chapter 6, 18 - 21

The Healing of a deaf Man

And as Jesus was going into a certain Village, there met him a Man who was deaf from his Birth. And he believed not in the Sound of the rushing Wind, or the Thunder, or the Cries of the Beasts, or the Birds, which complained of their Hunger, or their Hurt, nor that others heard them.

And Jesus breathed into his Ears, and they were opened, and he heard. And he rejoiced with exceeding Joy in the Sounds he before denied. And he said: 'Now I hear all Things.'

But Jesus said unto him: 'How sayest thou I hear all Things? Canst thou hear the Sighing of the Prisoner, or the Language of the Birds or the Beasts when they commune with each other, or the Voice of Angels and Spirits? Think how much thou canst not hear, and be humble in thy lack of Knowledge.'

Chapter 15, 8 - 10

Jesus rebuketh Cruelty to a Horse

And it came to pass that the Lord departed from the City and went over the Mountains with his Disciples. And they came to a Mountain, whose Ways were steep and there they found a Man with a Beast of Burden.

But the Horse had fallen down, for it was overladen, and he struck it till the Blood flowed. And Jesus went to him and said: 'Son of Cruelty, why strikest thou thy Beast? Seest thou not that it is too weak for its Burden, and knowest thou not that it suffereth?'

But the Man answered and said: 'What has thou to do therewith? I may strike it as much as it pleaseth me, for it is my own, and I bought it with a goodly Sum of Money. Ask them, who are with thee, for they are of my Acquaintance and know thereof.'

And some of the Disciples answered and said: 'Yea, Lord, it is as he saith, we have seen when he bought it.' And the Lord said again: 'See ye not then how it bleedeth, and hear ye not also how it waileth and lamenteth?' But they answered and said: 'Nay, Lord, we hear not that it waileth and lamenteth?'

And the Lord was sorrowful, and said: 'Woe unto you, because of the Dullness of your Hearts, ye hear not how it lamenteth and crieth unto the heavenly Creator for Mercy, but thrice woe unto him against whom it crieth and waileth in its Pain.'

And he went forward and touched it, and the Horse stood up, and its Wounds were healed. But to the Man he said: 'Go now thy Way and strike it henceforth no more, if thou also desireth to find Mercy.'

And seeing the People come unto him, Jesus said unto his Disciples: 'Because of the Sick, I am sick; because of the Hungry, I am hungry; because of the Thirsty, I am athirst.'

He also said: 'I came to end the Sacrifices and Feasts of Blood, and if ye cease not offering and eating of Flesh and Blood, the Wrath of God shall not cease from you, even as it came to your Fathers in the Wilderness, who lusted for Flesh, and they ate to their Content, and were filled with Rottenness, and the Plague consumed them.'

Chapter 21, 1 - 8

I believe, a Man
who can be heardless
against a
faithful Animal,
will never be
righteous
against
his own Kind,
and if one
is ever given
a Choice,
it is better
to be too gentle
than to be too harsh.

Antonia Katharina Tessnow
Bolonka Zwetna aus dem Alten Jagdhaus

Friedrich the Great

All Creatures on Earth love, suffer and die just like us; so they are Beings equal to us, put to Live by our Creator. They are our Brothers and Sisters.

St. Francis of Assisi

Antonia Katharina Tessnow
Bolonka Zwetna aus dem Alten Jagdhaus

Jesus setteth free the caged Birds

And as Jesus was going to Jericho, there met him a Man with a Cage full of Birds which he had caught, and some young Doves. And he saw how they were in Misery, having lost their Liberty, and moreover being tormented with Hunger and Thirst.

And he said unto the Man: 'What doest thou with these?' And the Man answered: 'I go to make my Living by selling these Birds which I have taken.

And Jesus said: 'What thinkest thou, if another, stronger than thou, or with greater Craft, were to catch thee and bind thee, or thy Wife, or thy Children, and cast thee into a Prison, in order to sell thee into Captivity for his own Profit, and to make a Living?

Are not these, thy fellow Creatures, only weaker than thou? And doth not the same God, our Father and Mother, care for them as for thee? Let these, thy little Brethren and Sisters, go forth into Freedom and see that thou do this thing no more, but provide Honestly for thy Living.

And the Man marvelled at these Words and at his Authority, and he let the Birds go free. So when the Birds came forth, they flew unto Jesus and stood on his Shoulder and sang unto him.

And the Man inquired further of his Doctrine, and he went his Way, and learnt the Craft of making Baskets, and by this Craft he earned his Bread, and afterwards he broke his Cages and his Traps, and became a Disciple of Jesus.

Chapter 41, 1 - 6

Jesus releases the Rabbits and Pigeons

It came to pass one Day, as Jesus had finished his Discourse in a Place near Tiberias where there are seven Wells, a certain young Man brought live Rabbits and Pigeons, that he might have to eat with his Disciples.

And Jesus looked on the young Man with Love and said to him: 'Thou hast a good Heart and God shall give thee Light, but knowest thou not that God, in the Beginning, gave to Man the Fruits of the Earth for Food, and did not make him lower than the Ox, or the Horse, or the Sheep, that he should kill and eat the Flesh and Blood of his fellow Creatures?

Ye believe that Moses indeed commanded such Creatures to be slain and offered in Sacrifice and eaten, and so do ye in the Temple, but behold! A greater than Moses is herein and he cometh to put away the bloody Sacrifices of the Law, and the Feasts on them, and to restore to you the pure Oblation and unbloody Sacrifice as in the Beginning, even the Grains and Fruits of the Earth.

Of that which ye offer undo God in Purity shall ye eat, but of that Kind which ye offer not in Purity shall ye not eat, for the Hour cometh when your Sacrifices and Feasts of Blood shall cease, and ye shall worship God with a holy Worship and a pure Oblation.

Let these Creatures therefore go free, that they may rejoice in God and bring no Guilt to Man. And the young Man set them free, and Jesus broke their Cages and their Bonds.

But lo, they feared lest they should again be taken captive, and they went not away from him, but he spake unto them and dismissed them, and they obeyed his word and departed in Gladness.

Chapter 28, 1 - 6

And the Birds gathered around him,
and welcomed him with their Song,
and other living Creatures
came unto his Feet,
and he fed them,
and they ate out of his Hands.

Chapter 34, 3

Jesus rebuketh the thoughtless Driver

And Jesus was travelling to Jerusalem and there came a Camel heavy laden with Wood. And the Camel could not drag it up the Hill whither he went for the Weight thereof, and the Driver beat him and cruelly ill-treated him, but he could make him go no further.

And Jesus, seeing this, said unto him: 'Wherefore beatest thou thy Brother?' And the Man answered: 'I knew not that he is my Brother, is he not a Beast of Burden and made to serve me?'

And Jesus said: 'Hath not the same God made of the same Substance the Camel and thy Children who serve thee, and have ye not one Breath of Life which ye have both received from God?

And the Man marvelled much at this Saying, and he ceased from beating the Camel, and took off some of the Burden and the Camel walked up the Hill as Jesus went before him, and stopped no more till he ended his Journey.

And the Camel knew Jesus, having felt of the Love of God in him. And the Man inquired further of the Doctrine, and Jesus taught him gladly and he became his Disciple.

Chapter 31, 12 - 16

The Healing of a blind Man

And there was a certain Man who was blind from his Birth. And he denied that there were such Things as Sun, Moon and Stars, or that Colour existed. And they tried in vain to persuade him that other People saw them; and they led him to Jesus, and he anointed his Eyes and made him to see.

And he greatly rejoiced with Wonder and Fear, and confessed, that before he was blind. And now, after this, he said: 'I see all, I know everything, I am God.'

And Jesus again said unto him: 'How canst thou know all? Thou canst not see through the walls of thine House, nor read the thoughts of thy fellow Men, nor understand the Language of Birds, or of Beasts. Thou canst not even recall the Events of thy former Life, Conception, or Birth.

Remember with Humility how much remains unknown to thee, yea unseen, and doing so, thou mayest see more clearly.

Chapter 41, 10 - 13

Jesus denounces Cruelty

As Jesus passed through a certain Village, he saw a Crowd of Idlers of the baser Sort, and they were tormenting a Cat which they had found and shamefully treating it. And Jesus commanded them to desist and began to reason with them, but they would have none of his Words, and reviled him.

Then he made a Whip of knotted Cords and drove them away, saying: 'This Earth, which my Father and Mother made for Joy and Gladness, ye have made into the lowest Hell with your Deeds of Violence and Cruelty.' And they fled before his Face.

But one more Vile than the Rest returned and defied him. And Jesus put forth his Hand, and the young man's Arm weathered, and great Fear came upon all; and one said: 'He is a Sorcerer.'

And the next Day the Mother of the young Man came unto Jesus, praying that he would restore the withered Arm. And Jesus spake unto them of the Law of Love and the Unity of all Life in the one Family of God. And he also said: 'As ye do in this Life to your fellow Creatures, so shall it be done to you in the Life to come.'

And the young Man believed and confessed his Sins, and Jesus stretched forth his Hand and his withered Arm became whole, even as the other. And the People glorified God, who had given such Power unto Man.

Chapter 24, 1 - 5

The Transfiguration on the Mount
The Giving of the Law

And Jesus said unto them: 'Behold a new Law I give unto you, which is not new but old. Even as Moses gave the Ten Commandments to Israel after the Flesh, so also I give unto you the Twelve Commandments for the Kingdom of Israel after the Spirit.

For who is the Israel of God? Even they, of every Nation and Tribe, who work Righteousness, Love and Mercy and keep my Commandments, these are the true Israel of God.' And standing upon his Feet, Jesus spake, saying:

'Ye shall not take away the Life of any Creature for your Pleasure, nor for your Profit. nor yet torment it.

Ye shall not steal the Goods of any, nor gather Lands and Riches to yourselves, beyond your Need or Use.

Ye shall not eat the Flesh, nor drink the Blood of any slaughtered Creature, nor yet any Thing which bringeth Disorder to your Health or Senses.

Ye shall not bear false Witness against any, nor wilfully deceive any by a Lie to hurt them.

Ye shall not do unto Others, as ye would not that Others should do unto you.

Ye shall cherish and protect the Weak, and Those who are oppressed, and all Creatures that suffer wrong.

Ye shall work with your Hands the Things that are good and seemly; so shalt ye eat the Fruits of the Earth, and live long in the Land.

Ye shall purify yourselves daily and rest the seventh Day from Labour, keeping holy the Sabbaths and the Festival of your God.

Ye shall do unto Others as ye would that Others should do unto you.'

Excerpts from the Chapters 46, 7 - 21

Blessed are ye
who abstain from all things
gotten by Bloodshed and Death,
and fulfill all Righteousness:
Blessed are ye,
for ye shall attain to Beatitude.

Chapter 20, 8

Jesus condemneth the ill-Treatment of Animals

And some of his Disciples came and told him of a certain Egyptian, a Son of Belial, who taught that it was lawful to torment Animals, if their Sufferings brought any Profit to Men.

And Jesus said unto them: 'Verily, I say unto you, they who partake of Benefits which are gotten by wronging one of God's Creatures, cannot be Righteous, nor can they touch holy Things, or teach the Mysteries of the Kingdom, whose Hands are stained with Blood, or whose Mouths are defiled with Flesh.

God giveth the Grains and the Fruits of the Earth for Food and for righteous Man. Truly there is no other lawful Sustenance for the Body.

The Robber who breaketh into the House made by Man is guilty, but they who break into the House made by God, even of the least of these, are the greater Sinners. Wherefore I say unto all who desire to be my Disciples: keep your Hands from Bloodshed and let no Fleshmeat enter your Mouths, for God is just and bountiful, who ordaineth that Man shall live by the Fruits and Seeds of the Earth alone.

But if any Animal suffer greatly, and if its Life be a Misery unto it, or if it be dangerous to you, release it from its Life quickly, and with as little Pain as you can. Send it forth in Love and Mercy, but Torment it not; and God, the Father and Mother, will shew Mercy unto you, as ye have shown Mercy unto Those given into your Hands.

And whatsoever ye do unto the Cast of these, my Children, ye do it unto me. For I am in them and they are in me. Yea, I am in all Creatures and all Creatures are in me. In all their Joys I rejoice, in all their Afflictions I am afflicted. Wherefore I say unto you: Be ye kind one to another, and to all the Creatures of God. '

Chapter 38, 1 - 6

The Truth maketh free

And certain of the Elders and Scribes from the Temple came unto him saying: 'Why do thy Disciples teach Men that it is unlawful to eat the Flesh of Beasts though they be offered in Sacrifice as by Moses ordained.

For it is written: God said to Noah: The Fear and the Dread of you shall be upon every Beast of the Field, and every Bird of the Air, and every Fish of the Sea, into your Hand they are delivered.'

And Jesus said unto them: 'Ye Hypocrites, well did Esaias speak of you, and your Forefathers, sayings: This People draweth nigh unto me with their Mouths, and honour me with their Lips, but their Heart is far from me, for in vain do they worship my Teaching and Believing, and Teaching for divine Doctrines - the commandments of Men in my Name - but to satisfy their own Lusts.

As also Jeremiah bear Witness when he saith, concerning blood Offerings and Sacrifices: I, the Lord God, commanded none of these Things in the Day that ye came out of Egypt, but only this I commanded you to do: Righteousness, walk in the ancient Paths, do justice, love Mercy, and walk humbly with thy God.

But ye did not hearken to me, who in the Beginning gave you all Manner of Seed, and Fruit of the Trees and seed having been for the Food and Healing of Man and Beast.' And they said: 'Thou speakest against the Law.'

And he said against Moses: 'Indeed I do not speak nor against the Law, but against them who corrupted his Law, which he permitted for the Hardness of your Hearts.

But, behold, a greater than Moses is here!' And they were wrath and took up Stones to cast at him. And Jesus passed through their Midst and was hidden from their Violence.

Chapter 51, 12 - 18

The Cleansing of the Temple

And Jesus said unto them: 'Take these Things hence: Make not my Father's House an House of Merchandise. Is it not written: My House is a House of Prayer, for all Nations? But ye have made it a Den of Thieves, and filled it with all Manner of Abominations.'

And he would not suffer that any Man should carry any Vessel of Blood through the Temple, or that any Animals should be slain. And the Disciples remembered that it was written: Zeal for thine House hath eaten me up.

Chapter 71, 3 - 4

By the Shedding of Blood of Others is no Remission of Sins

Jesus was teaching his Disciples in the outer Court of the Temple and one of them said unto him: 'Master, it is said by the Priests that without shedding of Blood there is no Remission. Can then the Bloodoffering of the Law take away Sin?'

And Jesus answered: 'No Bloodoffering, of Beast or Bird or Man, can take away Sin, for how can the Conscience be purged from Sin by the Shedding of innocent Blood? Nay, it will increase the Condemnation.

The Priests indeed receive such Offering as a Reconciliation of the Worshippers for the Trespasses against the Law of Moses, but for Sins against the Law of God there can be no Remission, save by Repentance and Amendment.'

Chapter 33, 1 - 3

And after seven Days, again, his Disciples were within the upper Room; then came Jesus, the Doors being shut, and stood in their Midst and said: 'Peace be unto you.' And he was known unto them in the holy Memorial.

And he said unto them: 'Love ye one another and all the Creatures of God. Yet I say unto you: Not all are Men, who are in the Form of Man. Are they Men or Women in the Image of God, whose Ways are Ways of Violence, of Oppression and Wrong, who choose a Lie rather than the truth?

Nay, verily, till they are born again, and receive the Spirit of Love and Wisdom within their Hearts. Then only are they Sons and Daughters of Israel, and being of Israel they are Children of God. And for this cause came I into the World, and for this I have suffered at the Hands of Sinners.

Chapter 88, 1 - 3

The Teaching of Cruelty in Animals

And as Jesus was going with some of his Disciples, he met with a certain Man who trained Dogs to hunt other Creatures. And he said to the Man: 'Why doest thou thus?' And the Man said: 'By this I live, and what Profit is there to any in these Creatures? These Creatures are weak, but the Dogs they are strong.'

And Jesus said: 'Thou lackest Wisdom and Love. Lo, every Creature which God hath made hath its End and Purpose, and who can say what good is there in It? Or what Profit to thyself, or Mankind?

And, for thy Living, behold the Fields yielding their Increase, and the fruit-bearing Trees and the Herbs; what needest thou more than these, which honest Work of thy Hands will not give to thee? Woe to the Strong, who misuse their Strength, woe to the Hunters for they shall be hunted.'

And the Man marvelled, and left off training the Dogs to hunt, and taught them to save Life rather than destroy. And he learned of the Doctrines of Jesus and became his Disciple.

Chapter 14, 6 - 8

Animals, our Brothers and Sisters

And as Jesus entered into a certain Village he saw a young Cat which had none to care for her, and she was hungry and cried unto him, and he took her up, and put her inside his Garment, and she lay in his Bosom.

And when he came into the Village, he set Food and Drink before the Cat and she ate and drank, and shewed Thanks unto him. And he gave her unto one of his Disciples, who was a Widow, whose Name was Lorenza, and she took care of her.

And some of the People said: 'This Man careth for all Creatures, are they his Brothers and Sisters that he should love them?' And he said unto them: 'Verily, these are your fellow Creatures of the great Household of God, yea, they are your Brethren and Sisters, having the same Breath of Life in the Eternal.

And whosoever careth for one of the Least of These, and giveth It to eat and drink in its Need, the same doeth it unto me. And whoso willingly suffereth one of These to be in Want, and defendeth it not, when evilly entreated, suffereth the Evil as done unto me; for as ye have done in this Life, so shall it be done unto you in the Life to come.'

Chapter 34, 7 - 10

*

*

What is Truth?

Again, the Twelve were gathered together in the Circle of Palmtrees, and one of them, even Thomas, said to the other: 'What is Truth? For the same Things appear different to different Minds, and even to the same Mind at different Times. What, then, is Truth?'

And as they were speaking, Jesus appeared in their Midst and said: 'Truth, one and absolute, is in God alone, for no Man, neither any Body of Men, knoweth that which God alone knoweth, who is the All in All. To Men is Truth revealed according to their Capacity to understand and receive.

The One Truth hath many Sides, and one seeth one Side only, another seeth another, and some see more than others, according as it is given to them.

Behold this Crystal: How the one Light its manifest in twelve Faces, yea four times twelve, and each Face reflecteth one Ray of Light, and one regardeth one Face, and another another, but it is the one Crystal and the one Light that shineth in all.

Behold again, when one climbeth a Mountain and attaining one Height, he saith: This is the Top of the Mountain, let us reach it, and when they have reached that Height, lo, they see another beyond it until they come to that Height from which no other Height is to be seen, if so be they can attain it.

So it is with Truth. I am the Truth and the Way and the Life, and have given to you the Truth I have received from Above. And that which is seen and received by one, is not seen and received by another. That which appeareth true to Some, seemeth not true to Others. They who are in the Valley see not as they who are on the Hilltop.

But to each, it is the Truth as the one Mind seeth it, and for that Time, till a higher Truth shall be revealed unto the Same; and to the Soul which receiveth higher Light, shall be given more Light. Wherefore condemn not others, that ye be not condemned.

As ye keep the holy Law of Love, which I have given unto you, so shall the Truth be revealed more and more unto you. And the Spirit of Truth, which cometh from Above, shall guide you, albeit through many Wanderings, into all Truth, even as the fiery Cloud guided the Children of Israel through the Wilderness.

Be faithful to the Light ye have, till a higher Light is given to you. Seek more Light, and ye shall have abundantly; rest not, till ye find.

God giveth you all Truth, as a Ladder with many Steps, for the Salvation and Perfection of the Soul; and the Truth which seemeth to Day, ye will abandon for the higher Truth of the Morrow. Press ye unto Perfection.

Whoso keepeth the holy Law which I have given, the same shall save their Souls, however differently they may see the Truths which I have given.

Many shall say unto me: Lord, Lord, we have been zealous for thy Truth. But I shall say unto them: Nay, you have been zealous only, but that Others may see as ye see, and none other Truth beside. Faith without Charity is dead. Love is the fulfilling of the Law.

How shall Faith in what they receive Profit them, that does not hold it in Righteousness? They who have Love have all Things, and without Love there is nothing Worth. Let each hold what they see to be the Truth in Love, knowing that where Love is not, Truth is a dead Letter and profiteth nothing.

There abide Goodness and Truth and Beauty, but the greatest of these is Goodness. If any have Hatred to their Fellows, and harden their Hearts to the Creatures of God's Hands, how can they see Truth unto Salvation, seeing their Eyes are blinded and their Hearts are hardened to God's Creation?

As I have reveived the Truth, so have I given it to you. Let each receive It according to their Light and Ability to understand, and persecute not Those who receive It after a different Interpretation.

For Truth is the Might of God, and it shall prevail in the End over all Errors. But the holy Law, which I have given, is plain for all, and just and good. Let all observe it for the Salvation of their Souls.'

Chapter 90, 1 - 16

*

*

When will the Night end?

A wise Rabbi asked his Students the following Question: 'How does One define the Hour, when the Night ends and the Day begins?'

One of his Students answered: 'Maybe it is the Moment, when one can distinguish between a Dog and a Sheep?'

The Rabbi shook his Head.

'Or maybe than, when one can distinguish between a Date- and a Fig-Tree?'

The Rabbi shook his Head again.

'But when is it then?'

The Rabbi answered: 'It is then, when you look into the Face of another Person and there you recognize your Sister or your Brother. Until then, the Night is with us.'

From: Hasidic Tales

Heaven and Hell

A Man, his Horse and his Dog were traveling down a Road. When they were passing by a gigantic Tree, a Bolt of Lightning struck and they all fell dead on the Spot.

But the Man did not realize that he had already left this World, so he went on walking with his two Animals; sometimes the Dead take time to understand their new Condition...

The Journey was very long, uphill, the Sun was strong and they were covered in Sweat and very thirsty. They were desperately in Need of Water. At a Bend in the Road they spotted a magnificent Gateway, all in Marble, which led to a Square, paved with Blocks of Gold and with a Fountain in the Center, that spouted forth crystalline Water.

The Traveler went up to the Man guarding the Gate.

'Good morning.'

'Good morning,' answered the Man.

'What is this beautiful Place?'

'This is Heaven.'

'How good to have reached Heaven, we're ever so thirsty.'

'You can come in and drink all you want.'

And the Guard pointed to the Fountain.

'My Horse and my Dog are thirsty, too'

'So sorry, but Animals aren't allowed in here.'

The Man was very disappointed, because his Thirst was great, but he could not drink alone. He thanked the Man and went on his Way. After traveling a lot, they arrived exhausted at a Farm, whose entrance was marked with an old Doorway, that opened onto a tree-lined, dirty Road.

A Man was lying down in the Shadow of one of the Trees, his Head covered with a Hat, perhaps asleep.

'Good morning,' said the Traveler.

The Man nodded his Head.

'We are very thirsty – me, my Horse and my Dog.'

'There is a Spring over in those Stones,' said the Man, pointing to the Spot. 'Drink as much as you like.'

The Man, the Horse and the Dog went to the Spring and quenched their Thirst. Then the Traveler went back to thank the Man.

'By the way, what's this Place called?'

'Heaven.'

'Heaven? But the Guard at the marble Gate back there said that was Heaven!'

'That's not Heaven, that's Hell.'

The Traveler was puzzled.

'You've got to stop this! All this false Information must cause enormous Confusion!'

The Man smiled:

'Not at all. As a matter of Fact, they do us a great Favor. Because over there stay all those who are easily capable of abandoning their best Friends…'

by Paulo Coelho

'I will not enter Heaven,
if this Dog does not come with me',
said King Yudhistiras.
Indra, the God, spoke:
'Today you will win Immortality,
Salvation
and everlasting Bliss.
You do not commit a Sin,
if you leave this Dog behind.'
'No', Yudhistiras insisted,
'not for all Treasures in Heaven
will I let this Dog down,
that searched my Protection
and was loyally devoted to me.'

Mahabarata

National Epos of India in Hindu-Sanskrit.
Its most important Didactic Poem is the Bhagavadgita.
Originated around 400 B.C. to 400 B.C.
Considered the Author is Vjasa.

An Indian legend says:
When a human dies,
there is a bridge
they must cross
to enter into heaven.
At the head of the bridge
waits every animal
that human encountered
during their lifetime.
The animal,
based on what they know
of this person,
decide which humans
may cross the bridge ...
and which are turned away.'

That would be Karma at it's finest.

Antonia Katharina Tessnow
Bolonka Zwetna aus dem Alten Jagdhaus

www.antonia-katharina.de

www.bolonka-zucht.de

www.light-in-time.com

Youtube Channel:

*Antonia Katharina
aus dem Alten Jagdhaus*

More Publications by Antonia Katharina Tessnow

The Books of the Bible
as separate, single Books
in big Writing

Why the books of the Bible as separate singles? The reason is as simple as practical: Most of the time, the Bible in its entirety has a very small writing and is, therefore, hard to read. Even if the publication itself is as big as possible and the writing still hardly decent, it is practically impossible to carry around all day, ever since it is so heavy.

But the books of the Bible, published as single books, allows the writing to be nice and big and therefore easy to read. Instead of carrying a heavy, big book around, you can choose one book of your liking, light enough to put in every pocket and easy to read. This way you can read the Bible wherever you like. In other words: The translators made the Bible available, this version makes it possible to easily read it.

Additionally, the single and easy-to-read versions of the single, biblical books can serve as an entry into the most important book of all times. Also the different books can be given away as a present to friends, family and loved ones. The easy-to-read version of the Bible is not only perfect for all those, whose hearts the message of salvation already reached, but also for all those who did not yet dare to approach the Bible and possibly felt overwhelmed by the volume and length of it.

The message of the Holy Scriptures can be of great help and support, give confidence, bring hope, comfort you, show sympathy and give consolation, especially during times, when we need hope and consolation so very much.

Whoever is seeking for the way home should know, that it is always open and there for us. This way is shown and can be found through the Bible. By making the decision to open up for the message of the Holy Scriptures, many people, throughout centuries, have found salvation, safety, hope and peace. And that is true up to this day.

King James Version

Writing, Format, Layout, Punctuation Marks:
Antonia Katharina Tessnow

www.antonia-katharina.de

Holy Night
Silent Night

1943. It is Christmas. All around the world, children write diaries to somehow cope with the unbelievable experiences they are send through during wartimes and turmoil. The slightly older sister of Antonia Katharina`s mother is 9 years old when she describes the events of one single night through her childish eyes. A destiny that leaves deep impressions on ones soul and won`t leave anyone untouched.

A wonderful reminder of the peaceful times we are allowed to live in today.

Antonia Katharina Tessnow is the daughter of a former East Prussian Family who came to Germany after World War I. Her grandparents settled in Berlin but had to flee the city together with their children after their apartment building was bombed and completely destroyed during the last year of World War II. They returned many years later to Berlin, but even though Antonia Katharina was born there, she never felt at home in this city. Today she lives in the countryside of Mecklenburg-Vorpommern.

Madras
Magic of the Palm Leafs

The Palm Leaf Library - Thousands of years old and an unsolved secret until today. The mystery of this place is the key subject of 'Madras'. The true story evolves around one of the greatest secrets of mankind.

I have been there. I left my small hometown near Berlin and discovered a legend which says, that every life story is written on a palm leaf; every life story? No, but the live story of all those people, who will undergo the long travel to one of the libraries and search for it. That is what I have done.

And this is, what I have found.

People who have read this book:

'A fascinating book. Whoever wants to find the answer to the question: How many lives do we have? will find it here.'

Günther Prinz, Managing Director and Chief Editor of 'Bild', Germany.

'So there is my entire life written on a Palm Leaf in Madras! This book completely changed my understanding of time and space.'

Fritz Bloomberg, Ex-Vicepresident Burda Press, New York

'Mind blowing! The ideal book for everybody who wants to learn about the unbelievable truth behind our existence.'

Gregor Tessnow, Germany

Author of the bestseller and the script of 'Knallhart'

Die biblischen Bücher
als Einzelausgabe im Großdruck

*inklusive Übersetzungsalternativen aus
unterschiedlichen Quellen*

Warum Einzelausgaben der biblischen Bücher? Der Grund ist so einfach wie praktisch: Die Bibel hat auf Grund ihres vollen Umfangs, selbst bei großformatigen Ausgaben, zumeist eine sehr kleine Schrift und ist demnach entsprechend schwer zu lesen. Möchte man zudem die Bibel gerne mitnehmen, um unterwegs zu lesen, entscheidet man sich schnell dagegen, solch ein schweres Buch den ganzen Tag mit sich umherzutragen.

Einzelne Bücher der Bibel erlauben dagegen eine für die Augen angenehme Schriftgröße und erleichtern somit das Lesen erheblich. An Stelle eines umfangreichen, schweren Buches ist es nun möglich, einen Text Ihrer Wahl in leicht tragbarer Ausführung mitzunehmen. So kann die Bibel einfach unterwegs gelesen werden. Mit anderen Worten: Luther hat die Bibel zugänglich gemacht, diese Version macht sie mühelos lesbar.

Zudem eignen sich die einzelnen Bücher hervorragend als Einstieg in die Bibel sowie als Geschenk; nicht nur für Menschen, welche die biblische Heilsbotschaft bereits erreicht hat, sondern auch für alle, die sich noch nicht an die Heilige Schrift heranwagten oder sich von dem Gesamtumfang der Bibel möglicherweise überfordert fühlen.

Die Botschaft der Bibel kann eine große Hilfe und Stütze sein, Zuversicht schenken, Hoffnung machen und uns trösten, gerade in einer Zeit, in der wir des Trosts so sehr bedürfen.

Wer den Weg nach Hause sucht, der soll wissen, dass er offen steht. Dieser Weg wird in der Heiligen Schrift gewiesen. Mit der Entscheidung, sich für die Botschaft der Bibel zu öffnen und diesen Weg zu gehen, haben unzählige Menschen seit Jahrhunderten ihr Heil gefunden. Und das bis zum heutigen Tag.

Übersetzung nach Martin Luther, 1545

Schriftsatz, Layout, Formatierung:
Antonia Katharina Tessnow

www.antonia-katharina.de

Heilbehandlungen für Dich und Dein geliebtes Tier

Erinnere Dich
an Deine verborgenen Fähigkeiten

Heilende Fähigkeiten wohnen in uns allen. Nicht nur in wenigen Auserwählten, sondern auch in Dir. Dieses Buch ist eine Erinnerung an all das, was Du kannst. Es beschreibt unterschiedliche Möglichkeiten, wie Du Deine heilenden Fähigkeiten nutzen und in Form von Heilbehandlungen einsetzen kannst - zum höchsten Wohle von Dir, Deinem geliebten Tier und Deinem geliebten Nächsten.

Antonia Katharina Tessnow studierte ganzheitliche Naturheilmedizin für Mensch und Tier, erlangte ihre internationale Heilerlaubnis an der int. Universität in Colombo und ist Doctor of Acupuncture und Homeopathy des Medicina Alternativa Institutes der Devi Clinic und Faculty of Integrated Medicine. Sie absolvierte eine mehrjährige Ausbildung am Institut für Emotionale Prozessarbeit, deren wesentliche Inhalte aus psycho-energetischen Prozessen, direktem Channeling und der Arbeit mit Informationsstrukturen im morphogenetischen Feld bestand. Während ihres 3-jährigen Indienaufenthaltes spezialisierte sie sich auf das Auslesen karmischer Lebensaufgaben und leitete Rückführungen in frühere Leben.

Bolonka Zwetna

*Von der Empfindsamkeit der Hundeseele
und der Liebe, die sie schenkt*

Dieser kleine Ratgeber soll nicht nur zum allgemeinen Verständnis der Beziehungen von Hunden zu uns Menschen beitragen, sondern vor allem den Menschen in seiner Seele berühren. Neben kurzen Überblicken über Rassestandard, Ernährung, Fellpflege und Haltung führt die Autorin den Leser in die facettenreiche Welt der Hundeseele, die voll tiefer Empfindsamkeit ist und niemanden unberührt lässt, der die Fähigkeit besitzt, zu fühlen.

Antonia Katharinas Liebe gilt seit jeher den Tieren. Viele Jahre war sie hauptberuflich in der Reiterei tätig bevor sie Heilpraktik, ganzheitliche Psychologie und Tierheilpraktik studierte. Seitdem widmet sie ihr Leben den Kleinhunderassen im Allgemeinen und dem Bolonka Zwetna im Speziellen. Neben ihrer schriftstellerischen, musischen und tierheilpraktischen Arbeit hat sie sich auf die Auftragsmalerei von Tierfotos spezialisiert und betreut ihre kleine Rassehundezucht der 'Zarenhunde aus dem Alten Jagdhaus'.

Die Hundezucht 'aus dem Alten Jagdhaus'
präsentiert sich unter

www.bolonka-zucht.de

Kommunikation mit Tieren

ein Essay

Tierkommunikation ist keine Kunst, die nur wenigen Auserwählten vorbehalten ist, sondern eine Fähigkeit, die in jedem von uns schlummert und uns allen innewohnt. Es ist nichts, was man lernen muss, sondern es ist etwas, woran man sich erinnern kann, wenn man dafür bereit ist. Dieses kleine Büchlein beschreibt in kurzen, aufeinander aufbauenden Abschnitten die Kommunikation mit Tieren. Es soll dabei helfen, sich an seine ursprünglichen Fähigkeiten zu erinnern und sie wieder nutzbar zu machen; es soll ein Wegweiser sein und zeigen, dass jede Begegnung eine Aufgabe für uns bereit hält, für die es immer eine Lösung gibt und an der wir wachsen können. Alles hat einen Sinn und es lohnt sich, darauf zu vertrauen. Selbst wenn wir ihn manchmal nicht gleich verstehen.

Textauszug: 'Jede Kommunikation ist individuell. Jede Verbindung, jedes Karma einmalig. Manchmal sind die Tiere überhaupt erst dafür da, um dem Menschen die gefühlte, intuitive Wahrnehmung und Kommunikation zu erschließen. Es ist ein Gewinn für alle, wenn der Mensch beginnt, eine Verbindung zu seinem Tier und damit zu sich selbst herzustellen, sich seinen Themen und deren Botschaften zu öffnen und von ihnen zu lernen. Wenn du dazu bereit bist, das Tier in seiner Ganzheit zu erkennen und als gleich-wertig zu schätzen, wenn du dich auf dein Ganz-Sein einlässt und dem Tier genauso erlaubst, es selbst zu sein, wie es das Tier dir erlaubt, dann entsteht wahre Verbundenheit. Wenn du über die weit verbreiteten Trainingsmethoden der Dominanz und der autoritären Kontrolle hinauswächst und dich dem tieferen Sinn einer Begegnung zuwendest, wenn du versuchst zu erkennen, was dein Gegenüber dir beibringen will, dann beginnt die Kommunikation mit deinem Tier.

Der Hund -
Das unbekannte Wesen

Was Sie tun können,
damit Ihr Hunde Sie liebt

Ein Leitfaden zur Eingewöhnung
des Hundes in ein neues Heim

Nach langjähriger Erfahrung als Hundezüchterin, Hundefriseurin, Youtuberin und Autorin sind mir viele Menschen und noch mehr Fragen begegnet, aus denen dieser Ratgeber entstand.

Nach bestem Wissen und Gewissen habe ich viele Antworten auf die mir begegneten Fragen sowie meine Erfahrungen und Erkenntnisse aufgeschrieben - *für Menschen wie Sie.* Für Menschen, die sich wagen, das große Abenteuer einzugehen, einer Hundeseele ihr Herz zu öffnen.

So hoffe ich inständig, dass ich Ihnen mit diesem Büchlein helfen kann, das Richtige zu tun, eine gute Fühlung zu Ihrem neuen Begleiter aufzunehmen und einen Beitrag zu mehr Verständnis zwischen der Menschen- und der Tierwelt leisten zu können. Meine tiefste Sehnsucht ist eine friedliche und tier-liebende Welt, in der wir Menschen unserer Verantwortung den Tieren und der Natur gegenüber gerecht werden, die uns in diesem einen, wohl wichtigsten Leitsatz überliefert ist:

'Seid niemandem etwas schuldig, außer, dass ihr euch untereinander liebet. Denn wer den anderen liebt, der hat das Gesetz erfüllt.'

aus dem Römerbriefen 8, 13

CD s by Antonia Katharina Tessnow are only available
through *amazon.com*

Books are available in every Bookstore

CD s by Antonia Katharina Tessnow are only available through *amazon.com*

Books are available in every Bookstore

Celtic Spirit

Eine Reise in die Tiefen
zeitloser keltischer Weisheit

In den Kulturen aller Zeiten findet man Spuren von der ursprünglichen Verbundenheit zwischen Mensch, Welt und Universum. Nicht nur bei den Kelten, sondern überall schien der Geist des Einklanges in der einen oder anderen Weise wirksam zu sein. Das *Einssein mit Allem*, woraus auch der Keltische Spirit hervorging, schien in uriger Zeit auf der ganzen Welt präsent und Grundlage jeder Form der Wahrnehmung.

Möge 'The Celtic Spirit' eine Idee davon geben, wie man über das Erfühlen der Bäume eine Verbindung zum Leben herstellt, wie sich die einzelnen Bäume anfühlen, warum sie bestimmten Zeitabschnitten im Jahr zugeordnet wurden und was sie mit diesen unterschiedlichen Zeitqualitäten gemein haben.

Und möge dieses Büchlein Inspiration für all diejenigen sein, die sich nicht nur ein ganzheitlicheres Verständnis mit der Natur wünschen, sondern sich auch nach einer tieferen Verbundenheit mit dem Leben sehnen.

Madras

Zauber der Palmblätter

Die Palmblattbibliotheken: Tausende Jahre alt und bis heute ein ungelöstes Rätsel. Das Geheimnis dieses Ortes ist das Thema dieses Buches. Die Geschichte dreht sich um eines der größten Rätsel der Menschheit.

Eine Reise führte mich dort hin. Ich habe meine kleine Heimatstadt verlassen um der Sagenumwobenen Legende auf den Grund zu gehen, die besagt, dass dort alle Lebensgeschichten aller Menschen niedergeschrieben sind; allerdings nur von denjenigen, die sich aufmachen, um danach zu suchen.

Eben das habe ich getan.

Und dies ist es, was ich gefunden habe.

**Dieses Buch
liegt in deutscher und englischer Fassung vor.**

Menschen, die dieses Buch gelesen haben:

"Ein interessantes Buch. Wer will, findet die Antwort auf die Frage: Wie viele Leben hat ein Mensch?"
Günther Prinz, Publizist, ehemaliger Chefredakteur der 'Bild', Deutschland

"Da steht also mein ganzes Leben auf einem Palmenblatt in Madras. Dieses Buch hat mein Verständnis von Raum und Zeit grundlegend verändert."
Fritz Bloomberg, Ex-Vizepräsident Burda Media, New York

"Ein außergewöhnliches Lesevergnügen, das meine Sicht auf die Welt verändert hat."
Gregor Tessnow, Schriftsteller und Drehbuchautor

Sternenstaub am Horizont

oder

Breakable - Zerbrechlich

der Fall

zwischen Selbstwert und Vernichtung

'Es gibt Geschichten im Leben, die hätte man lieber nicht erlebt.' Diese Aussage trifft auf viele Ereignisse zu. Doch meist ist diese Aussage nur auf den ersten Blick wahr; schaut man tiefer und geht der Frage nach: *Was hat mir dieses Ereignis zu sagen?*, oder: *Was hat mich dieses Ereignis zu lehren?*, wird oft der tiefere Sinn einer Erfahrung offenbar.

Nicht nur die Geschichte, die in dem Roman **Breakable - Zerbrechlich** verarbeitet ist, war eine dieser Erfahrungen, sondern auch all das, was um den Roman herum geschah. Vordergründig ein Thriller, hintergründig eine wertvolle Lektion über Selbstwert und Zerstörung.

Was geschieht, wenn der Selbstwert fehlt? Welche Auswirkungen hat das Fehlen von rechtzeitig gesetzten Grenzen? Und wohin kann einen der Weg führen, wenn man entscheidende Lebensthemen hat lösen können?

Durch den Roman veranschaulicht die Autorin nicht nur diese Problematiken, sondern bietet im zweiten Teil eine psychoanalytische Draufsicht, Aussichten für Betroffene sowie Lösungsansätze. Ein unumgängliches Buch für jeden, der schon einmal an seinem Selbstwert zweifelte und hofft, einen soliden Weg zur eigenen, inneren Wertschätzung zu finden.

Weiß Du,
was Du mit Dir trägst?

Eine Entscheidungshilfe
für Tattoo und Motiv

Was für Wirkungen auf Dich und welche Auswirkungen auf Dein Leben kann eine Tätowierung haben? Wie weitreichend können Veränderungen, wie tief Seelenschmerzen sein, die eine unbedachte Tätowierung möglicherweise mit sich bringt? Wie wichtig sind die Auswahl des Motivs und des Tätowierers?

Antonia Katharina Tessnow ging durch die dunkle Erfahrung einer vorschnellen Entscheidung und obendrein eines schlecht gestochenen Tattoos. Fast zwei Jahre ihres Lebens kostete sie die Wiederherstellung ihres Armes, für den sie sich täglich schämte. Ihre Leidensgeschichte beschrieb sie in dem ersten Teil des Buches 'Tattoo - Laser - Cover Up - Wenn der Traum zum Albtraum wird'. Für alle, die hoffentlich nicht vor dem Lasern und Covern stehen, sondern vor der einmaligen Entscheidung zu einer neuen Tätowierung, veröffentlicht sie nun den erweiterten und überarbeiteten zweiten Teil und bietet damit allen Tattoo-Freudigen einen Ratgeber und eine Entscheidungshilfe.

‚Frage Dich, was Du mit Dir tragen willst, bevor Du Dir mit einer falschen Entscheidung eine Bürde auflastest, die Du zu tragen nicht vermagst.‘

CD s by Antonia Katharina Tessnow are only available
through *amazon.com*

Books are available in every Bookstore

HAIR

Alles über alternative Haarpflege

HAIR - Alles über alternative Haarpflege, ist ein heilpraktisches Sachbuch. Es gibt in den einleitenden Kapiteln einen Überblick über die Inhaltsstoffe in herkömmlichen Shampoos und Duschgels und wie schädlich synthetisch hergestellte Chemikalien in der täglichen Anwendung auf Haut und Haaren sind. Des weiteren wird auf die Langzeitschäden eingegangen, die sich durch den dauerhaften und wiederholten Kontakt mit diesen Chemikalien ergeben können.

Der Hauptteil des Buches zeigt Alternativen zu herkömmlichen Produkten auf, die leicht umzusetzen und anzuwenden sind. Es wird auf komplizierte Anwendungstechniken verzichtet und ganz gezielt die Einfachheit der Methoden betont und in den jeweiligen Anwendungsbeschreibungen dargelegt. Alle alternativen Methoden zur Haut- und Haarreinigung sind von mir persönlich im Selbstversuch getestet, für jeden Interessierten leicht nachvollziehbar und die entsprechenden reinigenden Substanzen leicht erhältlich.
Im letzten Teil des Buches wird auf die Lebensweise, die Ernährung, Öle, Haarbürsten und Tipps und Tricks eingegangen, die langfristig und nachhaltig für gesunde und volle Haare sowie für gesunde, vitale und frische Haut sorgen.

Ziel dieses Buches ist es, das Bewusstsein für den Umgang mit unserem Körper, unserer Umwelt und damit unserer Gesundheit zu schärfen.

Stille Nacht, Heilige Nacht

Erinnerungen an einen Heiligen Abend
in den letzten Tagen des zweiten Weltkriegs

eine Kurzgeschichte

Diese Geschichte
liegt in deutscher und Englischer Fassung vor.

Über das Buch:

1943. Es ist Weihnachten. Schon damals schrieben
Kinder Tagebücher, um die unfassbaren Erlebnisse,
die in Worten kaum wiederzugeben sind,
festzuhalten. Die ältere Schwester von Antonia
Katharinas Mutter ist neun Jahre alt, als sie durch ihre
kindlichen Augen die Ereignisse einer Nacht
beschreibt, die tiefe Eindrücke hinterlassen und
niemanden unberührt lassen. Eine wunderbare
Erinnerung daran, in was für friedlichen Zeiten wir
heute leben dürfen.

Über die Autorin:

Antonia Katharina Tessnow ist die Tochter einer
ehemals ostpreußischen Familie, die nach dem ersten
Weltkrieg nach Deutschland kam. Ihre Großeltern
ließen sich in Berlin nieder, mussten jedoch aus der
Stadt fliehen, nachdem ihr Wohnhaus im letzten Jahr
des zweiten Weltkrieges zerbombt und komplett
zerstört wurde. Viele Jahre später kehrten sie nach
Berlin zurück. Obwohl Antonia Katharina dort
geboren ist, fühlte sie sich in dieser Stadt jedoch nie
heimisch. Heute lebt sie auf dem Lande am Rande der
Mecklenburgischen Schweiz.

CD s by Antonia Katharina Tessnow are only available
through *amazon.com*
Books are available in every Bookstore

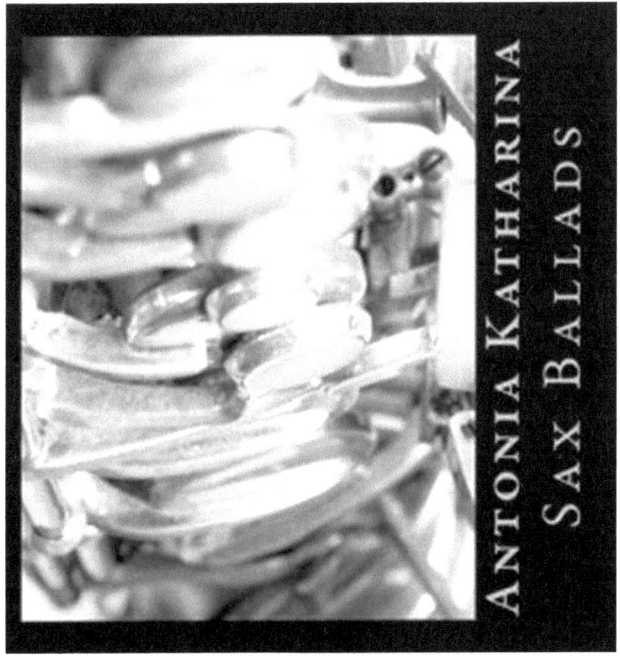

Tattoo – Laser – Cover Up

Wenn der Traum zum Albtraum wird

Sowohl das Tätowieren als auch das Lasern ist nicht nur ein Eingriff in deinen Körper, sondern auch in deine Persönlichkeit und dem daran gekoppelten Gefühl, dir selbst gegenüber. Tätowieren verändert einen Menschen; mitunter hat diese Veränderung weitreichende Folgen und hinterlässt tiefe Spuren in deiner Seele. Festzustellen, dass dir das langersehnte Tattoo nicht gefällt oder gar misslungen ist, ist zudem eine schmerzliche Erfahrung, für die es wenig Helfende und Mitfühlende gibt.

Dieses Büchlein soll nicht nur eine Hilfestellung für Betroffene sein, sondern auch die Gedanken derer anregen, die mit der Idee spielen, sich unter die Nadel zu legen. Nicht nur meine eigenen Erfahrungen rund um das Thema Tattoo – Laser – Cover Up sind hier offengelegt, sondern es wurde auch ein Blick in all die Seelenschmerzen und inneren Qualen gewährt, die mit solchen Erfahrungen verbunden sind.

Jede Krise enthält eine Chance, weswegen die Chinesen dafür ein und dasselbe Wort verwenden. Die Chancen dieser Krise sind die daraus entsprungenen, weiterführenden und sehr hilfreichen Gedanken sowie all die wichtigen Überlegungen zum Tätowieren allgemein, die dir hoffentlich helfen mögen und die du unbedingt anstellen solltest, bevor du eine Entscheidung triffst, die dich in jedem Fall für dein Leben zeichnen wird.

Breakable - Zerbrechlich

Der Skandalroman aus Mecklenburg

Dieser Psychokrimi hat in der Region, in der es erschien, für so viel Wirbel gesorgt, dass sogar die Presse in die Geschichte eingestiegen ist. Anfeindungen, Intrigen und Klagen finden nicht nur im, sondern fanden auch um das Buch herum statt. Näheres ist einzulesen auf dem Blog

breakablezerbrechlich.wordpress.com

Klappentext:

Eine Frau aus der Stadt. Ein kleines Dorf. Eine alte Köhlerkate, traumhafte Umgebung und idyllische Umgebung. Nicolas Leben könnte nicht friedlicher sein. Eines Tages begegnet sie einem Bauern aus der Nachbarschaft. Es ist Liebe auf den ersten Blick. Als diese von dem Mann mit der unverwechselbaren Stimme auch noch erwidert wird, scheint ihre Welt perfekt.
Doch Nicolas Glück ist nur von kurzer Dauer. Trug und Lüge lauern hinter jeder Ecke. Gerade als sie beginnt, das Ausmaß des Bösen zu entdecken, tun sich Abgründe auf, in die sie niemals hätte schauen dürfen.

Nach einer wahren Begebenheit.

'In ihrem spannenden Roman voller überraschender Volten und psychologischer Abgründe begegnet der Leser Figuren, die er seit Langem zu kennen glaubt.'

Henrik Leschonski, Lektor

Nichts geschieht umsonst auf dieser Welt

der Fall

Breakable - Zerbrechlich

die Anhänge

Zwar gilt schon der Roman *Breakable - Zerbrechlich* als psychologisches Lehrstück, doch erst die Anhänge machen die ganze Bedeutungstiefe der Geschichte erfahrbar. Wie wichtig Selbstwert für das eigene Leben ist wird kaum irgendwo deutlicher als im Buch Breakable. Wie wichtig die Liebe zum eigenen Leben und zu sich selbst ist, kaum irgendwo nachvollziehbarer als in diesem Buch.

Antonia Katharina Tessnow gibt mit den Anhängen nicht nur Einblicke in die Hintergründe, sondern offenbart auch die psycho-logischen Zusammenhänge zwischen fehlendem Selbstwert und der daraus resultierenden Zerstörung des eigenen Lebens. Warum erlauben wir anderen das permanente überschreiten unserer Grenzen? Und warum ist es lebens-wichtig, unsere Grenzen zu wahren, den eigenen Wert zu erkennen und unser Potential zu entfalten?

Nichts geschieht umsonst auf dieser Welt eröffnet ganz neue Perspektiven, zeichnet Lösungswege und gibt Hoffnung. *'Liebe deinen Nächsten **wie dich selbst'** bleibt somit kein leerer Satz, sondern wird zur gelebten Realität, sobald Deine Liebe nicht mehr nur die anderen, sondern auch Dich selbst meint.

Winston

Eine Pferdebuch-Trilogie für Jugendliche

Der große Sammelband mit allen 3 Bänden

Ein Fohlen erblickt die Welt

Die große Show

Nichts ist unmöglich

Winston Band I

Ein Fohlen erblickt die Welt

Die zwölfjährige Juna, die durch tragische Ereignisse viel zu schnell erwachsen geworden und ihrem Alter weit voraus ist, wünscht sich nichts sehnlicher, als ihrem derzeitigen Leben zu entkommen. Durch die Tragik ihrer Lebensumstände findet sie unerwartet einen Verbündeten, der ihrem Leben plötzlich eine ganz neue Perspektive gibt. Das Schicksal stellt sie vor große Herausforderungen und sie begreift schnell, dass Glück und Unglück manchmal näher beieinander liegen, als erwartet.

Antonia Katharina Tessnow, ehemalige Berufsreiterin, trainierte in einem renommierten Sportstall in Schleswig-Holstein Dressurpferde aller Klassen, bevor sie ins Berliner Olympiastadion wechselte. Dort arbeitete sie 6 Jahre lang als Landesverbandstrainerin des Modernen Fünfkampfes, beritt die Verbandspferde und unterrichtete die Disziplin Springreiten. Die Autorin hat eine Pferdebuch-Trilogie geschaffen, die ergreifend, anrührend und authentisch zugleich ist. Winston ist nicht nur ein Buch für Pferdefreunde, sondern auch für all diejenigen, die nichts mit Pferden zu haben, sich aber gerne von packenden und herzerweichenden Geschichten zwischen Menschen und Tieren mitreißen lassen.

"Die Autorin schrieb dieses Buch mit Sachverstand, Empathie und Fantasie. Die spannende Geschichte ist nicht nur etwas für eine Pferdebegeisterte, sondern auch für mich, als ehemaliger Bereiterlehrling und Gruppenleiterin eines Kinderheims."
Marie-Louise Ludwig

Winston Band II

Die große Show

Juna hofft noch immer, irgendwann einmal einen Platz im Leben zu finden, der sicher ist. Während die große Show für viel Aufregung sorgt, entwickelt sich das alte Gestüt, in all seiner Friedlichkeit, nach und nach zum unvergesslichen Ort ihrer Sehnsucht und in ihren stillen Augenblicken gibt es nichts, was ihr fehlt.

Die ehemalige Berufsreiterin und Landesverbandstrainerin des Modernen Fünfkampfes, Antonia Katharina Tessnow, ist 1975 in West-Berlin geboren. Sie sehnte sich ihre ganze Kindheit und Jugend nach einem Leben auf dem Land, weg vom Lärm der bedrängenden Stadt, die an der Mauer endete und die für sie, als junges Mädchen, unüberwindbar war.
Sie hat eine Pferdebuch-Trilogie geschaffen, die nicht nur tief berührend und authentisch ist, sondern all die Sehnsucht nach Sicherheit und Heimat widerspiegelt, die sie selbst einst in sich trug. Winston ist nicht nur ein Buch für Jugendliche, Pferdefreunde, Kenner und Liebhaber, sondern auch für alle, die sich gern von herzerweichenden und anrührenden Geschichten des Lebens mitreißen lassen.

'Beim Lesen der Winston-Trilogie fühle ich mich in die Reiterzeit meiner Jugend zurück versetzt und erlebe durch die Bücher die Atmosphäre der Ställe, den Umgang mit den Pferden und das Flair des Reiterlebens wieder, als wäre ich dabei.'
Bettina Wild, Diensthundeführerin, Tierkommunikatorin und Leiterin des Projektes: Landschaftspflege mit Ziegen, Schafen und Alpakas.

Winston Band III

Nichts ist unmöglich

Juna begreift immer mehr, dass es die Sicherheit, nach der sie sich sehnt, im Leben nicht geben kann. Alles kann in jedem Augenblick anders sein, als erwartet. Sie versteht, dass die Welt der Pferde auch andere Seiten hat und nicht jeder Mensch die Tiere so sehr liebt, wie sie. Wird sie das Schlimmste verhindern können? Steht ein Abschied bevor? Wird Winston überleben?

Antonia Katharina Tessnow, ehemals Berufsreiterin und Ausbilderin, führt heute eine kleine Hundezucht der Schoßhunderasse Bolonka Zwetna und hat ihr Leben vollends den Tieren verschrieben, die sie über alles liebt. Winston, ihr letztes langjähriges Berittpferd in der Landesreitschule am Berliner Olympiastadion, sein einmaliger Charakter und seine leidvolle Geschichte, spiegeln sich in der Winston-Trilogie wider.

'Winston lehrte mich mehr über Menschlichkeit, Charakterstärke und Unduldsamkeit gegenüber Lieblosigkeiten aller Art, als jedes andere Wesen, dem ich je begegnet bin. Möge er in diesen, nach ihm benannten Büchern weiterleben, und möge die Botschaft seines Lebens nie verhallen.'

Antonia Katharina Tessnow